Noah's Story

Published in Nashville, Tennessee, by Oliver-Nelson Books, a division of Thomas
Nelson, Inc., Publishers, and distributed in Canada by Lawson Falle, Ltd.,
Cambridge, Ontario.

ISBN 0-8407-3417-4

Manufactured in Singapore.

1 2 3 4 5 6 7 — 97 96 95 94 93 92

Noah's Story

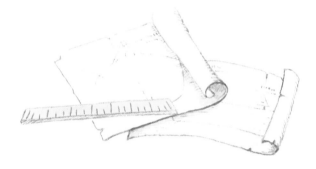

Halcyon Backhouse

Illustrated by
Jenny Press

A Division of Thomas Nelson Publishers
Nashville

God was very sad.
The people He had made
chose to hate Him.
On top of that,
they hated each other.
Only Noah was good.

God spoke to Noah.
"I will end these people.
Make a ship out of good timber."
Noah cut some trees.
His three sons helped him.

God told Noah how to make the ship.

It was very big.

It had three decks and a roof.

It had a lot of rooms.

All the people made fun of Noah.

"You are crazy," they said.

"Where is the water?"

God said,
"Get seven pairs of
all clean animals.
Get one pair of
all unclean animals.
Take them all on the boat.
Get plenty of food."
And Noah did what God said.
"What is that crazy Noah up to?"
the people asked.

Noah went into the ship.
He took his wife.
He took his sons
and their wives.
And God shut the door.
Then the wind came up.
The wind blew clouds
across the sky.
Drops of rain began to fall.
But Noah was safe.

The rain fell.
It made pools on the ground.
The pools became lakes.
The lakes became a sea.
And the ship floated on the sea.
The sea was gray.
The sky was gray.
And the rain fell.
The rain fell for forty days.

But God did not forget Noah.
One day, the rain stopped.
After a long time
the water went down.
And the boat got stuck on a mountain.
Noah sent out a raven.
He never saw it again.

Then Noah sent out a dove.
It did not find a place to rest.
So it came back.
After a week he sent it out again.
All day he waited.

The dove came back with a leaf
in its beak.
At last the flood had gone!

Noah waited one more week.
Then he sent the dove out again.
The dove found a home on land.
It did not come back.
So Noah took off the roof
and looked out.
He saw thick mud.
It was wonderful.

God said, "You can all get out now."
God put a rainbow in the sky.
He said, "This rainbow is My promise.
I will not flood the world again."
And Noah and his family praised God.